SOCIAL LIVES OF
GORILLAS

Rachel M. Wilson

Rourke
Educational Media

rourkeeducationalmedia.com

ANIMAL BEHAVIORS

Scan for Related Titles
and Teacher Resources

Teaching Focus:

Fluency: Encourage extensive reading and use specific methods, such as timed readings, and partner reading to stimulate growth in fluency.

Before Reading:

Building Academic Vocabulary and Background Knowledge

Before reading a book, it is important to set the stage for your child or student by using pre-reading strategies. This will help them develop their vocabulary, increase their reading comprehension, and make connections across the curriculum.

1. Read the title and look at the cover. *Let's make predictions about what this book will be about.*
2. Take a picture walk by talking about the pictures/photographs in the book. Implant the vocabulary as you take the picture walk. Be sure to talk about the text features such as headings, Table of Contents, glossary, bolded words, captions, charts/diagrams, and Index.
3. Have students read the first page of text with you then have students read the remaining text.
4. Strategy Talk – use to assist students while reading.
   - Get your mouth ready
   - Look at the picture
   - Think…does it make sense
   - Think…does it look right
   - Think…does it sound right
   - Chunk it – by looking for a part you know
5. Read it again.
6. After reading the book complete the activities below.

Content Area Vocabulary
Use glossary words in a sentence.

belch
bond
flees
gestures
grieving
tension

After Reading:

Comprehension and Extension Activity

After reading the book, work on the following questions with your child or students in order to check their level of reading comprehension and content mastery.

1. *What do the different noises and sounds gorillas make mean?* (Summarize)
2. *What is a group of gorillas called?* (Asking questions)
3. *What is the role of a silverback in a troop?* (Text to self connection)
4. *After reading the book, what do you think about gorillas?* (Summarize)

Extension Activity

Gorillas communicate using gestures, body postures, sounds, and by slapping their chests. Some gorillas living in captivity have even been taught sign language. With the help of an adult, go online and print out a sign language template. Make copies and give them to some of your friends. Practice and learn the alphabet and other symbols and communicate with your friends without making a sound!

TABLE OF CONTENTS

Troops   4

Gorilla Talk   7

Sweet and Shy   18

Photo Glossary   22

Index   24

Websites to Visit   24

About the Author   24

TROOPS

Gorillas depend on one another. They live in central Africa in social groups called troops. Troops have two to 30 (or more) members.

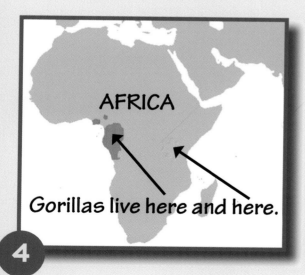

AFRICA

Gorillas live here and here.

Gorillas use sounds and **gestures** to share their emotions and intentions. This communication keeps gorilla troops happy and healthy.

Humans and gorillas are closely related. Gorillas, chimpanzees, and humans all have more in common with each other than with orangutans.

5

Each troop needs a silverback. This strong male protects his family. Troops include females, their young, and sometimes other silverbacks.

GORILLA TALK

Gorillas often show their teeth in greeting. This tells others "I mean no harm." Gorillas show affection by grooming. They

comb hair and pick out bugs. Weaker gorillas groom the silverback. This keeps them on his good side.

Gorillas wear a special face for play. This open mouth with teeth looks like a smile. Playful gorillas bow to the ground and touch a friend. This says, "Play with me!"

Young gorillas chuckle, pant, and grunt in play. They wrestle, chase, and make up games. Play burns off **tension**. It also helps gorillas **bond**.

Sometimes play turns rough. Then chuckles turn into grunts.

Silverbacks sometimes make peace between other group members. They break up fights and scold others.

Tense gorillas use grunts to stop fights. Mothers use them to correct their young. A nervous gorilla may pant. Annoyed gorillas stare and growl. This says, "Back off!"

Baby gorillas cry like humans. They even throw temper tantrums. This shows anger, discomfort, or fear.

Adult gorillas scream in fear. But some threats cause silence. This can happen when humans try to kill gorillas. The troop quietly **flees**.

Angry silverbacks are show-offs. They hoot, beat their chests, and charge. This noisy show may prevent a fight.

Gorillas use nature in creative ways. Western lowland gorillas use water for splash displays, which can be seen from far away.

Sad gorillas whine and cry.
When one gorilla dies, others try to wake
him. **Grieving** gorillas may stay with a
body for days.

SWEET AND SHY

Before building nests for the night, gorillas share happy sounds. They hum. They sing. They even make purrs called **belch** sounds.

Shy and gentle gorillas share much with humans. Yet, we are their biggest threat. Gorillas need our help to survive.

PHOTO GLOSSARY

belch (belch): A belch is a burp. When gorillas are happy, they make rumbling purrs that sound like human belches.

bond (bahnd): To bond is to come together. When social animals bond, they feel connected.

flees (fleez): An animal that flees is running away, often when scared or threatened.

gestures (JES-churz): Gestures are signals made with the body. Like humans, gorillas use gestures to communicate.

grieving (GREEV-ing): Grieving is feeling sadness after a death or other loss.

tension (TEN-shuhn): Tension is a feeling of nervousness or tightness, often when something bad is about to happen.

Index

communication 5
fear 12, 13
gestures 5
grieving 17
grooming 7

play 8, 9, 10
silverbacks 6, 11, 15
sounds 5, 18
troop(s) 4, 5, 6

Websites to Visit

http://kids.nationalgeographic.com/animals/
    mountain-gorilla
http://kids.sandiegozoo.org/animals/
    mammals/western-lowland-gorilla
http://gorillafund.org/learning_and_fun

Meet The Author!
www.meetREMauthors.com

About the Author

Rachel M. Wilson grew up in Alabama in a house full of animals. Rachel studied Theater at Northwestern University and Writing for Children & Young Adults at Vermont College of Fine Arts. Her debut novel *Don't Touch*, was published in 2014. These days, Rachel writes, acts, and teaches in Chicago, IL, where she shares a home with her best friend, a dog named Remy Frankenstein.

Edited by: Keli Sipperley
Cover design, interior design and art direction: Nicola Stratford
www.nicolastratford.com

Library of Congress PCN Data

Social Lives of Gorillas / Rachel M. Wilson
(Animal Behaviors)
ISBN 978-1-68191-702-3 (hard cover)
ISBN 978-1-68191-803-7 (soft cover)
ISBN 978-1-68191-900-3 (e-Book)
Library of Congress Control Number: 2016932580

Rourke Educational Media
Printed in the United States of America, San Jose, California

www.rourkeeducationalmedia.com

PHOTO CREDITS: Cover and title page © Guenter Guni; page 4 map © Zoologist, Wikipedia; page 4-5 © Photodynamic; page 6 © Hill2k, page 7 © Lorraine Logan; page 8 © Rob Hainer, page 9 © Inu; page 10-11 © Michael Shake, page 11 g dptro; page 12 © Joe McDonald, page 13 © Sergey Uryadnikov; page 14-15 © Tanya Puntti; page 16 Nick Dale, page 17 © Sergey Uryadnikov; page 19 © iPics; page 20 Martin P; page 22 top © Nejron Photo, bottom © Inu. All images from Shutterstock.com except Cover and title page istockphoto.com and ma page 4 Wikipedia,

Also Available as:
ROURKE'S e-Books